Happy
Easter
The festival of new life

Published in 2018 by Wayland
© Wayland 2016

Written by Joyce Bentley
Editor: Corinne Lucas
Designer: Ariadne Ward

A catalogue for this title is
available from the British Library

ISBN: 978 15263 0643 2

10 9 8 7 6 5 4 3 2 1

Wayland
An imprint of
Hachette Children's Books
Part of Hodder & Stoughton
Carmelite House
50 Victoria Embankment
London, EC4Y 0DZ

An Hachette UK Company
www.hachette.co.uk
www.hachettechildrens.co.uk

Printed in China

Contents

What is Christianity?

Christianity is an ancient faith. It is about 2,000 years old and has over 2.2 *billion* followers worldwide. Christians believe in one God who created Heaven and Earth.

The Bible is the Christian holy book. It is made up of 66 books and written by 40 authors, all telling the story of Christianity.

The Holy Spirit means that God is everywhere and in everything.

Christians believe that Jesus, the Son of God, died and then rose from the dead. They also believe that Jesus gave up his life so that humankind could start a new life with God, free from *sin*.

The golden domes of St Sophia's Cathedral in Kiev, Ukraine.

Being a Christian

There are three main groups of Christians: Roman Catholics, Orthodox and Protestant Christians. They have different traditions but they all believe in the *crucifixion* and *resurrection* of Jesus.

Churches are often built in the shape of a cross to remind Christians that Jesus died on the cross.

Churches are places where Christians go to worship together.

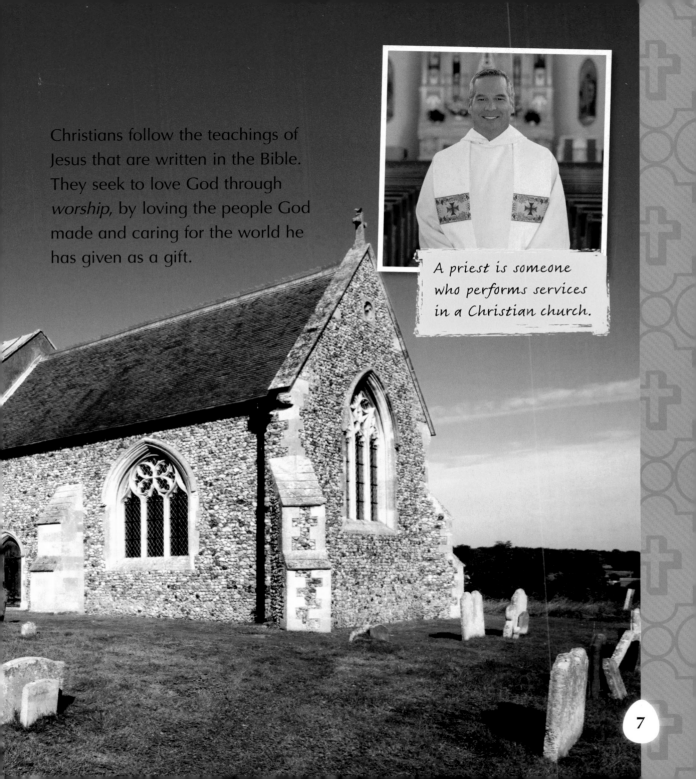

Christians follow the teachings of Jesus that are written in the Bible. They seek to love God through *worship,* by loving the people God made and caring for the world he has given as a gift.

A priest is someone who performs services in a Christian church.

What is Easter?

Easter is a festival that remembers the life and death of Jesus, on Easter Sunday. It is a joyful time for Christians around the world.

The week before Easter is called Holy Week. On Easter Sunday, Christians go to church to worship, sing hymns, follow processions and some people hunt for eggs.

Baby chicks are symbols of new life, often seen during the Easter season.

John 3:16
"For God so loved the world that he gave his one and only Son, that whoever believes in him shall not perish but have eternal life."

8

In Sicily, Italian locals hold a procession during Holy Week.

The Story of Easter

At Easter, Christians remember the story of Jesus's crucifixion and resurrection, and how he was sent to Earth to save humanity.

The Last Supper

On Palm Sunday, Jesus rode into Jerusalem with his 12 followers, known as disciples, to celebrate the Jewish festival, *Passover*. That night, Jesus had a last supper with his disciples. Jesus said, "This is my Body … this is my blood" as he handed them the bread and wine. He was saying goodbye to his friends because he knew that it was time for him to die, but that he would rise again.

Jesus knew that someone would *betray* him. When he went to the Garden of Gethsemane to pray and Judas appeared with Roman soldiers to arrest him, Jesus knew the betrayer was Judas. At a trial they sentenced Jesus to death for claiming to be the Son of God.

Jesus was forced to carry a heavy wooden cross on his back through the city to the top of a hill. There he was nailed to the cross and crucified. After he died, Jesus's body was placed in a *tomb* with a large rock covering the entrance.

The Crucifixion

The Resurrection

Two days later Jesus's friend, Mary Magdalene, went to visit the tomb and found that Jesus had risen from the dead. She was overjoyed and ran to tell his disciples. It proved that Jesus really was the Son of God. Jesus then told his disciples to spread the word of God, before being taken to *Heaven* by two angels.

11

Preparing for Easter

Christians remember the crucifixion of Jesus through artwork in churches and cathedrals.

Lent is the period of time before Easter. It lasts for 40 days, from Ash Wednesday to Easter Sunday (not including Sundays). During this time, Christians can give up their favourite foods and think about how Jesus *fasted* for 40 days.

The final week of Jesus's life is called Holy Week. It is a time when Christians think about the *sacrifice* that Jesus made for them.

Sundays are a day of celebration for all Christians as Jesus was resurrected on that day.

Holy Week Timeline

Palm Sunday

The day Jesus rode into Jerusalem and people laid palm leaves on the floor to welcome him.

Maundy Thursday

The last supper when Jesus told his disciples that he would leave.

Good Friday

When Jesus was tried by the Romans and crucified on the cross.

Holy Saturday

Followers of Jesus experience great sorrow for the death of their King.

Easter Sunday

Jesus rose from the dead and was discovered by Mary Magdalene.

An ancient tomb in Israel, similar to the one Jesus was buried in.

Celebrating Easter

Easter Sunday is a happy day for Christians as Jesus rose from the dead, showing that he had defeated even death. Many churches start Easter celebrations with a midnight service on Holy Saturday.

On Easter Sunday, Christians go to a morning service where they remember that God loves them so much that he gave up his only Son for them.

A child lights a candle to remember that Jesus brought light into the lives of millions of Christians.

Christians lining up for communion during Easter Sunday service.

On Easter Sunday, Christians say: "Christ is Risen", "Truly, he is risen".

Children and Easter

Children celebrate Easter by going to church and playing games on Easter Sunday. There may be Easter egg hunts, egg rolling competitions and craft activities.

Children at the yearly White House Easter egg rolling competition in Washington, USA.

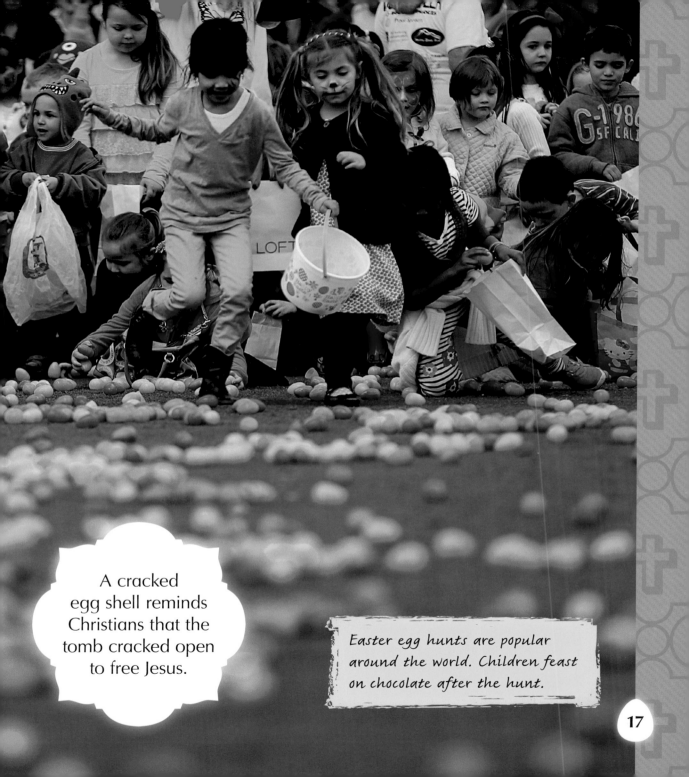

A cracked egg shell reminds Christians that the tomb cracked open to free Jesus.

Easter egg hunts are popular around the world. Children feast on chocolate after the hunt.

A Time for Feasting

Food plays a big part at Easter. Christians around the world have their own traditional recipes. Roast lamb and vegetables are commonly eaten as a main meal.

Each country bakes their own cakes and breads, such as Colomba di Pasqua in Italy, Pinca in Eastern Europe and Capirotada in Mexico.

The 11 marzipan balls on top of an Easter simnel cake represent the disciples, but not including Judas!

Kulich is often eaten in Russia and Bulgaria. It is a tall baked cake decorated with icing and sprinkles.

Hot-cross buns are a popular Easter treat in the UK. The cross reminds Christians of Jesus's crucifixion.

Tsoureki is a brioche-like bread decorated with red hard-boiled eggs.

Thinking About Easter

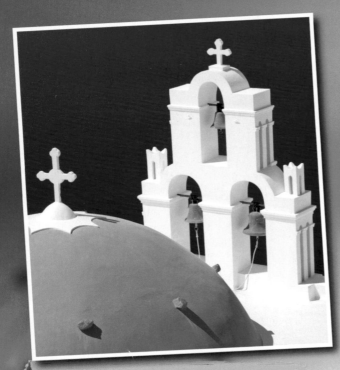

The cross is an important symbol for Christians of God's love and it is found on many buildings.

Christians believe that God gave his Son to bring forgiveness and hope into a sinful world. Because of this, Christians know that God loves them and this give them great hope for their lives ahead.

During Lent people give up their favourite foods (see page 12). Have you ever given something up for Lent? What would you give up?

resurrection hope forgiveness
crucifixion eggs disciples love
cross God Easter joy
new life Jesus spring tomb

This word cloud contains words that remind us of Easter. Can you think of any more words?

Decorate an Easter Egg

Painting eggs for Easter is a great activity for children of all ages. You can experiment with bright colours and different patterns.

Material
You will need some fresh eggs, acrylic paints, different sized brushes, a sponge, water and an egg box.

Getting Started
Ask an adult to hard boil the eggs. Once they are cooled you can paint them. Paint a background colour on the egg, doing of half the egg at a time and leave it to dry in an egg box after each layer of paint.

Once the egg is dry you can try different designs and patterns. Lightly dip a sponge into some paint and press it around the egg for a speckled effect.

Practise different techniques until you are confident to try more complex designs.

Use a few bright colours then add details, such as dots, stripes or flowers.

Another way to colour the eggs is to boil them in vinegar, then leave them in a bowl with food colouring. The eggs then absorb the coloured dye.

Glossary

Billion – a million millions

Betray – to double-cross someone to their enemy

Communion – a Christian service where bread and wine are shared

Crucifixion – the killing of Jesus on a cross

Fast – to not eat for a period of time

Heaven – a place where Christians believe God lives

Passover – A Jewish holiday

Resurrection – to return to life after death

Sacrifice – to give up something to help others

Sin – an offense against a religious law

Tomb – a large grave that can hold more than one body

Vatican – where the pope lives

Worship – to honor or respect (someone or something) as a god

Index